Manhandling the Deity

John F. Deane was born on  Poetry Ireland – the National Poetry *view* in 1979. He is the author of man ction. His poetry includes *Christ, n*)7), a collection translated into seve · *New and Selected Poems* (Carcanet, 2 published in French, Bulgarian, Romanian, Italian and Swedish translations. John F. Deane's prose works include two novels, *In the Name of the Wolf* (Blackstaff Press, 1999), published in German translation in 2001, *Undertow* (Blackstaff Press, 2002), and a collection of short stories, *The Coffin Master* (Blackstaff Press, 2000). In 1996 John F. Deane was elected Secretary-General of the European Academy of Poetry. The recipient of the O'Shaughnessy Award for Irish Poetry in 1998, and the Grand International Prize for Poetry from Romania in 2000, in 2001 John F. Deane was given the prestigious Marten Toonder Award for Literature. His poems in Italian, translated by Roberto Cogo, won the 2002 Premio Internazionale di Poesia Città di Marineo for the best foreign poetry of the year.

Also by John F. Deane from Carcanet

Toccata and Fugue: New and Selected Poems

JOHN F. DEANE

Manhandling the Deity

CARCANET

First published in Great Britain in 2003 by
Carcanet Press Limited
Alliance House
Cross Street
Manchester M2 7AQ

A CIP catalogue record for this book
is available from the British Library

ISBN 1 85754 638 5

The publisher acknowledges financial assistance
from the Arts Council of England

Set in Monotype Garamond by XL Publishing Services, Tiverton
Printed and bound by CPI Antony Rowe, Eastbourne

Give them eternal rest O Lord,
and let perpetual light shine over them

Mary, mother of us, where is your relief?
                                        (Hopkins)

Go,
it is the Mass

Contents

Old Red House

Swallows have taken over
the guts of the old red house, quickening
through the famished windows;

they have nested in the high
webbed corners of the stairwell, dropped
birdshit on the trodden carpet, feathers and

one tiny bird-foetus, soft-beaked
and naked. The winds go creaking
on the stairwell, sometimes half-banging

a half-hanging door half-to.
The rains are stripping down
the fleur-de-lys plum wallpaper;

in the kitchen, by the rusting Rayburn,
a rat is a leathern wallet
flat in the grime and rubbish,

while out in the hallway these
mirror-images: the couple, young, still whole,
admiring the foundations of their living –

and opposite: the God of ages, face
distorted, and slow dribbles of blood
onto the hallstand, frames and wainscotting.

The Rains Persisting

It has rained for days across the suburbs;
chalk games of the smaller children
have washed down into the gutters;

we have seen the dead laid out
in sheeted humps, the shrivelled young
stilled for the camera while they weep inwardly;

somewhere else mauled bodies
are being drawn up from wells.
I remember how we prayed for weather

during the old ceremonies, holding that God
intervenient in our concerns: migrations, meadows,
trawlers out on dramatic seas. The domains

of reason we claim ours though we may boast
rarely of them, while God's are the domains
of mystery, where he stays aloof, brooding perhaps

on man's catastrophies, and shedding tears.

Processional

They come, down country lanes, by alder, fuchsia, thorn,
or threading in through speed-ramp pockmarked streetways;
they are gathering already on the forecourt, gloved
hand clapping gloved hand against morning frost,

the men in dark wool coats, in tweeds and leathers,
the women dressed in their toned-down best, the frenzy
of living set aside – and pause awhile, as if there was a way
to postpone this morning's interview. Garrulous

at first under the porticoes, they grow nervous
till winter winds drive them inside, whispering
against sudden stillness. Along the roadside railings
an almost-hidden line of snowdrops stands

like tiny acolytes before the coming rubrics.
Always, for now, it is someone else, and someone else's
family suffering grief, in the Mercedes limousine
that turns at last, discretely, into chapel grounds.

Officium

Spare me Lord for my days burn off like dew.
What is man that you should magnify him;
why do you tender towards him your heart of love?
You visit him at dawn, touching him with dreams,
whisper to him at dusk, while the swings still shift
and soft rain falls on the abandoned frames.
Why have you made him contrary to you
that he learn baseness, anger and defeat
swallowing his own saliva in sudden dread?
Can you erase his sins, like chalk marks,
or place your angels as a fence about him?
The trees dreep softly, the attendants are gone home.
Today I will lie down in sand, and if tomorrow
you come in search of me, I am no more.

Mercy

Unholy we sang this morning, and prayed
as if we were not broken; crooked
the Christ-figure hung, splayed
on bloodied beams above us;

devious God, dweller in shadows,
mercy on us;
immortal, cross-shattered Christ –
your gentling grace down upon us.

Last night an old man pushed along the hill,
holding the bike from him lest it buck, and kick;
his hair straw-wisps in the breeze,
his hand on the chrome bar a yellow twig;

he mounted, warily, as a cowboy in our old films
mounted an unbroken stallion; a soiled
brown coat flapped against the cross-beam,
his route the longest distance between points

till he fell, bike and all, tumbling backside over bars
into the drain below Lineen's stores.
Mercy on us all, the afflicted ones.
But oh how we sang when he climbed onto the road

like a Signorelli figure in the resurrection of the dead.

Elliptic

A small meshed gate,
a hard-earth yard, hens important with the full
freedom of the house;

egg-woman, she was generous
with the flesh-browns, the buttermilk-whites,
her movements always

close to repose, like the imperceptible
elliptical motion
of the spheres;

birthed sons that were
hard-handed for hod and concrete, her space
poverty, and her time

labour. World, she said, goes on,
egg to chicken to egg –
and her thin hands

yanked life suddenly out of them.
Sons, to boys, to men; she cried
each time they left to build

Birmingham and Liverpool, they, too,
obedient to the laws of the world's orbit. *Kyrie
eleison.* Between times she tended

the graves of the parish, seasoning
loss with flowers, sheening –
with her dank sleeve, her chicken-wing

dusters – the incised names of those
who had migrated
to eternity.

Frenzy

A small row-boat on Keel Lake,
the water sluppering gently as he rowed,
the easy sh-sh-sshhhh of the reeds

as we drifted in, and all about us
tufts of bog-cotton like white moths,
the breathing heathers, that green-easy lift

into the slopes of Slievemore. All else
the silence of islands, and the awe
of small things wonderful: son,

father, on the one keel, the ripples
lazy and the surfaces of things unbroken.
Then the prideful swish of his line

fly-fishing, the curved rod graceful,
till suddenly mayfly were everywhere,
small water-coloured shapes like tissue,

sweet as the host to trout and – *by Jove!*
he whispered, old man astounded again
at the frenzy that is in all living.

Alice's Harbour Bar

Locked the office door behind him: cabbage
      green, paint like scabs on sunburnt skin;
           locking himself out from tedium.

Evening rain
      came in gusts off the Atlantic. He moved
           slowly across the yard; a little

shakily. *I confess* ...
      Settled to face
           recriminations; after such days he would need

redemption. How a man can hate
      himself, hate slippage in the war he wages,
           find it impossible to forgive

himself. Tang of sea-rot
      on the air; it would be easy, self-
           pitying, to lift the mind towards God.

*

We crossed the Liffey on O'Connell Bridge
speaking of Wittgenstein, Goethe, the Connaught Final;

I can remember
the silence of the river underneath us,

his stook of hair,
how he would live forever ...

*

Each day dawned with prayer
and each day died: Our
father. Give us this day, he'd say,

our daily dying.
He in his office,
with papers, notes, files, inks and dossiers;

rising with a sigh, reaching
for another man's avowed
income, expenditure. The value of a life

clinging to ink at the nib-tip.

*

The Morris Minor waited, glum and heavy;
       he choked it, rain all day
              persisting; gripped the driving wheel,

moved, cautiously, across the yard
       and out towards the road; sluggish, self
              and car. Turn right

for Alice's Harbour Bar. Left,
       for home. He knows again the sickening frisson
              of excitement: to be caulked

in companionable darkness, drink
       comforting, the world
              shaping itself to manageable forms: or face

reproach and silence, the harshest judgement
       in her sorrow, in the children's eyes
              watching him with barely hidden terror.

*

Waiting. Long past time. The gut
tightening. The clock
on the mantel ticked more loudly.

Their silence, their busying
was all their words. The mother
hurting for her daughter, the daughter

sensing how it rounds again
like the tide. Mutton
stewed on the glistening Aga; aprons

taken off, put on again. Love
scoured to a sheen till the small
faults appeared.

*

Outside our window the Scots pines hissed
in night winds off the sea; he drew the curtains,
sealing us in a yellow light; thrilled, we waited;
Bela, he told us, means beautiful, and she –

Our matt-painted walls were the steppes, the black
impossible eyes of a woman flared at us, we saw
the flanks of horses gleaming in the moonlight;
broad is the river Dnieper, he told us,

the proud wild goose glides swiftly over. Sometimes
we shivered as Mephistopheles approached,
or hearing Carmen's lovely laughter: *la fleur
que tu m'avais jetée dans ma prison* ...

How could we know, as he gathered us to sleep,
the nightmare of the tedium of his days?

*

He sat, under the nineteenth-century clock,
with its Roman numerals, its pendulum pulse;
tock, tock, tock, tock, tock,
each day configuring the same old grey
and brown discovery of what becomes –

discovered, only the past, the files of
yesterdays heavy with hand-smudged papers;
enthusiasm dead, like a small furred body
growing nasty in a corner, become
endurance, the wooden sag of a table

supporting dead weight; here were no
shifting constellations, no circling
dance of sun and moon and tide – only
the gathering of each day down to dust.

*

We moor on the shores of a vast ocean;
    north, south, north, south – timekeeping –
        the currents seethe through arches of a bridge;

the window of Alice's Harbour Bar
    watches out over the sound, the glass
        grimed with the spittle of wind and sea.

In the gloom the man's big fist
    gripped the pint of stout, his feet found purchase
        on the sawdust floor; he grows

confident here, out of it; (drinks); that we are all
    water, returning to the state of water,
        fluid and faithful to the watergod;

the old men bob their heads; they know
    the coarse weight of seaweeds, the grail
        warmth of whiskey piping their veins.

This is his moment, between-times, the soul
    swelling in celebration (drinks); the walls
        grey-drab, pocked floorboards uneven.

Like the deck of a trawler, yawing.

Alice has laughed her gruff, considerate laugh;
    stout arms akimbo on her mothering breasts
        she has seen it all before, and heard it,

the thirst, the collander
    emptiness being filled;
        she has held them, their strong hands

trembling, their minds grown friable
    as dried-out clay, their drowning cries
        audible to everyone but themselves.

*

I was sent in with messages;
I remember dust, a souring smell, men
big as shadows and leaning at me,
their teeth a seaweed brown but their hands

dry and callused where they touched; they were intent
as if embroiled in serious businesses.
He hoisted me, showing me off, onto the counter;
I felt the spillings cold on my bare hocks

and pulled to get away but his grip was fierce,
not to be broken by the puny boy he'd fathered.
At night we prayed, *Eternal rest
grant unto them, and let perpetual light* ...

I understood and, forehead pressed against the chair
I prayed for them, the souls in purgatory,
noisy, noisome, restless in the bleak light;
confess, be cleansed, seventy times a thousand times ...

*

Tears were blinding him. Rain on the windscreen.
        He raised his arm across his eyes. A shape
                suddenly out of the murk. He braked. Hit

the creature, hard, across the rump, felt
        the thud like rock on clay, the Morris
                sliding on the hissing surfaces, dreamlike

in a slow waltz, unstoppable. Silence then,
        control over his destiny withdrawn, his being
                held, irresistibly, out of the long flow.

Knock

We trudged round and round the old building
as if we were getting somewhere, our fingers
rambling round the beads, our heads
bowed against the petulant winds and rains.

We were an ancient people, our hearts
full of ancient gentility, unlovely
butterflies seeking a flame to burn against.
The end wall of the church, we were told,

and the inhospitable landscapes of the west
had flared with a heavenly light. We have since
learned to scoff at all such drollery, at the stalls
rife with the junk of old piosity. Today

ours is a swift, a rectilinear glide,
to wealth, wellbeing and ultimate contentment.
Sometimes I wonder, when that old, dim message
of peace and love and prayer and charity

fades under the groans of stalled traffic, if perhaps
the perfect pilgrimage is a circling,
or better yet a wilful stomping in place,
or best of all, eyes closed, attending, and standing still.

Seafarer

(a reading of the Anglo-Saxon poem)

I

May I relate a truthful tale from my life, tell
of a journey, how in long labour-filled days
I suffered whole hours of hardship, felt

bitter anguish, bore terrible anxieties,
was occupied so often in watches of the night
on a ship's prow in severe and pounding seas

when we tossed under cliffs and when my feet
were frozen and fettered with the chains
of frost. Cares festered in my heart and great

hunger came harrying my mind, oh I was a man
wearied by the sea. Still, how could you know –
or anyone who lives in luxury and ease on land –

how I, wretched and anxious, with the sea ice-cold,
must wander through winter on the exiles' trail,
far from my loving family, in misery untold,

icicles about me and showers of the sharpest hail;
the only sounds the sad echoing of brine
and the breaking surf. I'll have the swan's wail

for entertainment, the wearying gannet's whine,
curlews' calls in lieu of the laughter of men,
the seamew's cry in place of the pleasures of wine.

I remember tempests crashing on cliffs, the tern
was icy-feathered and often the eagle sang,
his feathers drenched with dew. None of my faithful kin

could comfort my soul in its distress. How wrong
it seems to you who live in the comfort of cities,
how little you know of journeys, terrifying, long;

when you're lazy, lusting for wine, how can you see
why I wearily pursue the ocean paths.

II

                            Out of the north
snow has fallen, frost is binding up the sea –

hail and freezing rain are falling on the earth;
once more my courage fails as the thought forms
that I must venture out across the currents, go forth

on the commotion of salt waves. My soul warns
that I set out far from here and seek the homes
of people unknown to me. There is no one born –

no one so blessed with goods, no youth so callow,
so bold and brave in action, nor close to the heart
of his leader, but knows anxiety before a journey, knows

it is the Lord's demand determines he must go;

the pleasures of music and laughter, the love of his wife,
the comforts of this world: all are weariness to his mind;
nothing holds the seafarer save the harshness of his life,

the eagerness he knows for the ocean, to be far from land.
Woods may grow green and blossom, buildings seem fair,
heath and field are beautiful, nature hastening to expand –

all that but stirs the soul determined still and eager
to set out on the journey a spiritual life demands.

III

The sad hail of the cuckoo, like a sacred harbinger,

stimulates the summer, the way seafaring sorrows
bring bitterness to the heart. How can the highborn know:
those couched in comfort: what certain men go through

who fare the farthest into areas of exile?
So now my own thoughts turn beyond known barriers,
wander widely out to the home of the huge whale,

to the very edge of earth, and longing leaves me
eager and hungry; the calls of that lonely bird
urge me irresistibly out on the way of the sea

because the joys of the service and love of the Lord
are dearer far to me than this dead life,
time transitory here on earth as any trysting word.

Earthly goods will not stand a man eternally; always
something takes him at the appointed time: disease
or age or violence will carry him away;

so, in proud assemblies nothing can equal praise
from the living, for those lordly men who have achieved,
before their death, their due of good works, whose days

passed magnanimously on earth, in spite of the malice
of enemies, whose bravery faced with evil is well known
and brings honourable mention to men's lips. And this

praise lives afterwards among the angels, in the glory
of eternal life, with hymns of joy among angelic hosts
for ever.

IV

Ages pass, so too the pomp and store

of earthly riches; no king, no emperor remains,
no generous patrons; each person must achieve
his own great and glorious deeds, must strive alone

for honour; gone are worldly joys, those hosts are gone;
the morally weak are with us still, living in the ease
of their feeble labours. Honour, integrity, have flown,

for the true grow wizened and wither as any on the face
of the earth, features grow pale, and the fever
of grief comes with grey hairs, with memories of great

and valued friends who have left the earth forever.
The flesh grows flaccid as life's tide ebbs away,
sweet things don't suit the palate, all tastes bitter,

see how hands stiffen, how thoughts go suddenly astray.
Though you build monuments of gold to his memory
your brother still must lie amongst the dead; and why

bury with him the treasures his busyness achieved,
what use such tatters and trinkets to a soul in sin,
what consolation, before God's terror, can gold be,

pitifully piled away during a life's long attrition?
The earth itself will crumble at the Creator's word,
who fixed the universe on immovable foundations,

who shaped the firmament, the sea, the whole world.
He is foolish who does not fear the Lord; death, too soon,
will fall on him. He who lives a humble life and good

is blessed; these favours fall on him from Heaven, too,
with grace and faith and all that's good, from God.
A man's mind must steer him strongly and stay true

to promises, he must fare honestly. And every man
must know moderation, avoid evil, always strive
to keep his will fixed firm as a rudder against sin.

Let us think then where our true home lies
and learn how we may sail thereto, and learn to win
God's grace against the fateful meeting where man's life

will be blessed by the Lord's love in the port of heaven,
by Him who has honoured us though we sin and sin again,
the Prince of Glory, the great Captain for ever. Amen.

The Emigrants

I woke to a fraught and un-
familiar darkness; I sensed
the simperings of drifting rain,
pre-dawn breezes in the pines;

while I slept it had begun already,
the creaking of a cart,
the slow-rhythm, dull, steady
hoof-beats of a horse;

I dreamed through that comfortless noise.
And heard them then outside our gate,
the urgent, hushed, voices,
nervous shiftings against the dark;

a woman's wail lifted high
in distress, like a furred animal
transfixed suddenly and I
was awake to the sound of the approaching

bus, its labouring through the gears to
stop. It stayed. Ticking.
I imagined the trunk, bulked and new,
tied round with fishing-rope,

how it was hoisted
up under tarpaulin on the bus roof;
then those awkward gestures and voices,
embarrassed kisses and knobbled words

like sand ramparts against a rising tide,
how the hurt was held back, the way
you hold your palm to your side
to contain the suffering. The bus

moved, loudly, labouring on the road
into silence. Silence. Then the creaking
of a cart, the same, slow rhythmic plod
of the hoof-beats of a horse.

Psalm

All night the coffin was a laid-down instrument
in the side-aisle; morning, and the old folk, waiting,
urge their rosaries, their knuckles hard as beads;
we have fallen still, they pray, in the care of truth
and what have we to show? Old bones, knotted.

In the sibilance of trestle-wheels the coffin comes
to take its place upon the podium; outside
it is spring, blossoms of the plum in a melody
of white. Lord you have touched and known us; we
have only old scores to settle, old drums to beat.

Father to Son

(a reading of the Latin poem of Colman, c. 800)

If then you are suddenly anxious to see
that gentle land, the refuge that we both share,
go quickly, don't feel restrained by any plea

of mine, nor hint of nostalgia in my prayer.
Why should I blame the tedium of a mind
grown dull; love of home wins out, and who would dare

deflect a lover? If Christ could redefine
my life's span, renew the vigour of my days,
bring back the flowering of my age, rewind

time to make these white hairs black: who says
I too would not be tempted? You must ignore
in your deep longing, an old man's sluggish ways;

remember Virgil who sang how old age bore
all away, slowed the blood and cooled the veins,
wearying the body and wasting out the store

of life's strengths; nor is there any heat remains
in dried-out flesh. The distances across the sea,
the dangers of rough shores, all that terrifies and strains

my heart. Let you, Colman, not hesitate, be
valiant against the waves, keeping in your heart
the thought of another Colman who is, at least, free

to give advice! Then listen, before we part,
be not distracted by the world's pomp, which blows
away like wind, or the way vain dreams start

and die, smoke trails to vapour, the river flows
ever more swiftly out to sea. For your care
centres there; go gladly; the Almighty knows

your longing; to the one Hope of life, my prayer
that he govern the temper of the waves, that his hand
calm the winds, that he take himself the helm, bear

you safely over the abyss until you land
on that loveliest of shores. Live happy there, my boy,
grow famed for your good living throughout all Ireland.

Joy all your days, and after, everlasting joy.

The Dead and the Undead of St Michan's

They attended us, like martyrs, for centuries
as if their bones were stone and their skin
cured leather. They stood like sand-shapes
abandoned by tides, their language courtesy

and silence. We were witnesses to patience,
withheld decay, to timekeepers tremulous
to be loosed onto the air; we shook hands
with Strongbow, Patrick, Jesus, Thor

and left again, awed, and less afraid.
But the cider-drinkers, the language-killers,
came at night from our impatient streets,
they heaped the bones into a pyre, and the skulls

void with a centuries' old screaming, till –
with a communal sigh – the ancients yielded
to the flames. Farewell, our old familiars,
our seafarers, our progenitors, our clowns.

In a Shop Window

He curls into a city doorway,
his night-home refrigerator packing cases,
his mattress last month's newspapers;

the clattering of footsteps past him has grown less,
chocolate wrappers whip in the wind and a can
dances passionately in the gutter;

shaven-headed and unshaven, he is a gathering
of man-stench and garbage smells;
his eyes are dried-out seeds and you look

quickly away. Sometime in the night one hand
will fall heavily out along the pavement, palm
upward to the stars, fingers bent so you can see

the perfect quarter-moons of his fingernails,
the lifeline like a contour map of the sky.
This is the very image of God's abdication,

foolish, unlovable, the sheen on glass
throwing back our appalled faces where we stand,
immersed in self as in lambswool coats, certain

of our place in the world, our destination.

The Pilgrim's Rest

In the Hauptplatz, old men
crediting themselves all-over children
go rollerblading by; you can mount

a yellow pony-train through the old quarter
as if you were a child still blessed
in your ignorance of everything;

bring, however,
your banker's card, your signature.
In the Hauptplatz

a person in God's care has found the shade
and a supply of last year's news;
around him floats

the aroma of mussels-cooked-in-wine, of dumplings,
of the fattened loins of swine,
where the solid-bellied ones, in floral shorts,

renege a while on their mortality
accepting the indulgence
of a kettle-bellied God;

seek out
the foothills of paradise, between noon and snoozing-time
and allow, insouciantly, the bill to climb.

Somewhere nearby
a town hall bell is ringing
a child's tune of all-is-well.

*

Every journey made
takes us to such places as if
they were a destination, but they are not;

we touch on them awhile
the way old uncle Noah's big adventure
dribbled out on Ararat, when he

and all his retinue
touched earth again, assuming
mortality overcome.

*

Like Gotland, in the dry grass,
where the stone ribs of a longboat lie
whose chief and crew, centuries ago, sailed

fiercely into dust; wild
strawberries flourish in the hold and breezes
in the high pines come gossiping; or here,

in Macedonia, the hermit's cave
high on the cliff face while amused goats
watch us labouring up the steps, where we light,

in the tightest of sandstone places,
tiny tapers to be our prayers and emerge again
startled by the bright lake below

and cowed once more by our naivety.

Nightwatch

In our suburban villages, our dormitory towns
we lie secure. But at the city's core
up and down the crack-tiled steps of the men's
shelter, they pass who could be minister

or president or priest – but are not;
in dust-striped suits and mismatched waistcoats
who could be civil servants – but are not;
greased and creased and ill at ease they ghost,

side-staggering, our streets, who might
be Plato, Luther, Hopkins but for some tiny thing
that slipped and shifted them a little to the side.
Their dream is a coin found under slanting

light, oblivion enough to damp down care
a while. But wish us all good health and reason
who wake sometimes, knowing we too have been
visited by importunate ghosts and have forgotten;

tell us what we dreamed, interpret for us the dream.

Between Clay and Cloud

I

Ascension Day. No matter. April rain,
the psalmody of blackbirds. We stand
gazing up to heaven while clouds darken
off the Irish Sea. Blossoms have blown
from the cherry trees and the cars slither
in a petal-slush. Hastening. Only a few
faithful elderly came to pray, knelt
dismayed in a church that groaned
like a storm-shaken ferry. That old God
is gone, and his Son, broken; a Spirit
pleads unheard under the clamour.
Yet once we stood in awe as hero Christ
lifted into glory the way those flick-
ering movies ended in the local hall.

II

I believe in God
self-broken and incomplete,
in the creating pulse of his self-regarding love

that spun the universe and its derivatives;
that he created man in his own image
self-broken and incomplete.

I believe in the mathematical necessities
of birth and suffering and suffering and death
ordered by the Father for our edification.

*

We are born to states of sin
because we are not God;
we are born broken

because we are.
We sport a cancer, erotic
orchid of the will; put forth

the blood-red sore of the ego-flower.
My sin: I believe that I exist;
forgive me, Father, my existence.

*

At the back of the church a wooden stairs
turned to the gallery; a window, frosted,
husks of flies, a woman's black silk glove;
you rose always into the unexpected.

Ascension Day, and the girls' choir singing;
how they watched and giggled, how they stared
when you passed with messages;
the mistress leading, *Holy God we praise*

Thy name. Alone then, on ordinary days –
to every echoing and unsettling sound –
you opened, guiltily, the old harmonium,
you worked your feet and heard the wind

fill its lungs with a laboured breathing;
you opened the stops, diapason, and played,
gamba, Johann Sebastian Bach, the way
you loved it; *Sleepers Awake!* and they did:

in the fair field of the chapel below you
they'd stir in pew and aisle or applaud
among the high beams and rafters, the music
asserting a fluid deity, decorous and flawed.

III

And in his only Son,
enigma, the Jesus-
word uttered
when he spoke

his impulsive foolishness;
creating power
become love become
man. A man, like men

broken.
After the measured
ballet of reason we step
on the ice of mystery.

*

We reach our hands in supplication;
ours the posture of ignorant attending,

the forked tree, the fists
flung out in surrender.

*

In the chemicals' fall,
in all this world's
manifold disasters I believe
that the rusting chains of history

bind his wrists. Though he waits removed
where we would draw him down to earth, he
hangs yet between clay and cloud
transfixed to stillness and drawing

all things to himself.
Every death coheres
like gore to his blanched flesh
where love became power again and God began

to find his own
healing. I believe in the Son,
self-
broken and complete.

*

We are a cold, dark-suited congregation
with our scents, our applied pigments
and dandruff on our Sunday collars;

some of us are old folks,
small now and blackened
like tree stumps after lightning;

sometimes the walls dripple with our sweat,
and the children cry out of long frustration;
sometimes the sun shines silently in

and the beauty of our confined spaces
shatters us into praise; sometimes,
when faith, like a firefly, comes glimmering.

IV

And in the Ghost, the aspiration,
breath of his utterance,
bolero of winds on the wild meadow,
frisson of wisdom along the spine;

stirrings on the landing of the brain,
shiftings in the stairwell of the soul;
he vibrates us with unheard music,
chorus of our waking and dirge

of our going down. I believe
in verses, the worked-for inspiration,
the enabling image and fortuitous conjunction;
the sudden startling flights like disturbed birds.

V

Ascension Day. We lined up in cloisters,
faithful, our reasoning willed to silence;
holding the black biretta, coracle
and tassel-sail of our believing. Spiritans.
Filing into choir on the wave-surge of the hymns,
breath of the organ sustaining us, and all the rituals.
Over bowed heads the Spirit hawed
like a hothouse breeze, and centuries of trust
hung as dust in the folds of our surplices.
I looked up then, and there was nothing: the priests
exotic shore-people signalling, tinkering
with exotic instruments. And the Spirit passed
in a slow rush, out the door where the people
moved in the rich, polluted air of the world.

*

He breaks the host, I hear the breast-bone
of a small bird snapping; he hoists the sweet-
blood chalice, I hear cries of distress
from a famished people. When we enter

it is the stone terminus of an underground
and we wait, in ranks, sway, sigh and leave
as if we had reached a destination. He was broken,
taken down, buried, grew whole again and won

authority over this flawed creation.
Give us this day our incentives;
fill us with goals though there is no goal;
give us this day our daily energy.

O broken God be with us always,
now, and to the end of time.

Officium

Spare me Lord for my days blow like smoke.
What is man that you should magnify him;
why do you tender towards him your heart of love?
You visit him at dawn, urging him into labour.
At dusk he's carried, weary, contented, home,
with *ignis fatuus* in its mocking jig behind him.
Why have you made him contrary to you
that he appropriate the world in hunger,
filling his belly full with all good things.
Can you erase his sins, scatter them like ash,
renew the heather plains he has destroyed?
The beasts sleep restlessly, the small stacks loom.
Today I will lie down in mould, and if tomorrow
you come in search of me, I am no more.

In a Time of Violence

These years, untimely nations like our own
have found a place in the encyclopedia
of tragedies: Timor, Chechnya, Kosovo;
two thousand years since the child-Christ's star

and still we are breaking one another's bones.
Swans, on the banks of the canal,
are factory workers on their coffee break,
down scattered about like bread offerings;

but out beyond the city's limits the water's
troubled: flaccid and water-weighted bodies
have been drawn out and laid
under plastic sheets: in our own back lanes

much precedented outrage. Who come to pray –
in a time of violence – present their words
like holed jars refusing to contain
expected consolations. Arthritic hands

offer the ordinariness of bread, the occasional
headiness of wine; wearying minds plead
for the sudden brilliance of the wings of angels
to lift the heart towards realms of peace. Detritus

gathers at the locks, plastics swollen with old air
and water. Today's offering: an average life,
ash from an average fire, and a small glass
of disturbed and disturbing faithfulness.

Magdalene

All day the daffodils and narcissi
have been struggling with winds and April drizzle;
the trees are bare, like a million refugees
whose hands are raised in supplication. We are held

in unnatural impetus again towards death,
watching ourselves kneel, and rise, and kneel again:
this is the wood of the cross, one arm bared.
Tonight, in the dim hours, at the corners

of boulevards, by streetlamps a woman drifts,
despondent, dress hiked; she smokes, waiting.
Once more we are drawing close to the end
of this impossible week when the God

broken again, repentant of his one deed,
offers himself forgiveness on the cross.
Occasional cars shift by, headlights dimmed and
these, too, are lives disturbed by the long grief.

We have set it up so often, remembering,
on the rough wood of the cross, the body bared, as if
after two thousand years we have learned
nothing. In the stilled church tonight everything

will be absence, and in the soul the old
despondency. *Father, forgive us*, forgiveness
at least being possible. Did she stand silent,
stricken, all tears spent, on the hill? The God

being absent, what is impossible is to offer
oneself forgiveness; and how could she know,
as she drifted through the dim hours before dawn,
she'd be the one to knock first on the tomb's door?

Woman

I Mother

I sing of a woman,
  The peerless one;
The King of all Kings
  She selected as son.

His coming so still
  Where his mother was,
Like the dew in April
  Lying on the grass.

His coming so still
  To his mother's bower,
Like the dew in April
  On the apple flower.

His coming so still
  Where his mother lay,
Like the dew in April
  On the blackthorn spray.

Woman and lover
  So special was she,
Never another
  God's mother to be.

(adapted from the late fifteenth-century poem)

II Nuptial

The first evening, and a room apart;
trout in the stream below, sated; stars
like silver moths flickering on the water;
somewhere, beyond the trees, a strong
soprano voice was singing requiem.
She was shy and eager, her mind
on the unguent that would make the first

entry easier. She was sand
as if the God had lain in sand,
shaping it, or water, displacing it, or air;
and her soft animal calls were of joy
as if you could take into your mouth
the wild thrush's song at dusk or allow
salmon-flesh to melt slowly on the tongue.

III   Niche

Stood, unreachable, in the wall
on the women's side,
effete in white, vapid
in blue; ideal woman, her small
feet crushing viperous jaws; sweet,
soft and acquiescent, the negative of female
while lily-flaccid candles fell
guttering at her feet.

IV   Spirit

Noon, and silence;
the blackthorns are a storm of blossoms, stilled;

on the branch-tips of the peach tree
the most delicate of growths

where blue tits dodge excitedly.
She has come

naked from the bathroom, her breasts
pout; stands

suddenly, as if she were not alone.
What is the angel but the shape of noon?

Conjunction of peace and beauty and the onward roll
lifting her soul to ecstacy that wills

God's presence be made actual in flesh.

V   Harbour

All day the porpoises
played jazz extempores across the bay,
drawing crowds over the sands
to the edge of wonder;

in the small harbour the *Maris Stella*
unloads this day's harvest:
crabclaws, mackerel, ray,
lobster and flop-fleshed dogfish;

men in yellow oilskins and green waders
stand like out-of-season daffodils,
fish scale, fish blood on deck and pier
and tourists hesitant and grimacing.

Listen! The gulls: *Dei mater alma*;
mother, kindly and nourishing sea.
Tonight the moon over the ocean
will lift its languorous saxophone solo.

VI   The Journey

Sometimes in the afternoons
they were naked under admitted sunlight,
hands and tongues rapid as lizards,

slow as the growth of lilies. This, too,
was incarnation, the third
presence. Weary then, and in pain,

the ground about her rough and broken,
the night sky clear and bitterful with stars,
the child within her bucking, her body

strained to bursting. Making the journey
beautiful, the rounding of the stars and of her pain
beautiful, and the irresistible

impulse of God within it, and everywhere.

VII On the Hobstone of Pain

Mary of graces,
      Mother of God's son,
O guide my path
      Till my life's done.

Guard and keep me
      From all that's foul,
Guard and keep me
      Both body and soul.

Guard and keep me
      On land, sea and air;
Guard and keep me
      On the hobstone of pain.

Angels watching
      Above my head,
God before me,
      God at my side.

(adapted from the Irish)

VIII Pietà

She is older now, has learned
not all see God in world and flesh;
old Jewish mother, she still slow-walks
in consciousness of the body's beauty;

sits always with another of her children,
her face lined where God's five fingers
have scraped along it; her son,
dead, has been laid again across her lap

more helpless than when he was a baby;
Chechen mother, her son embraced
in barbed wire; Iraqi, the body of her son
blackened by long-distance firepower;

yet she is glad, having him back,
would offer him again her breast,
to give him life; Albanian child, laid down
before the caterpillar wheels of tanks;

Ethiopian, paper package of bones
where the flies glut. He lies
as if he, too, were content. Jesus,
blood everywhere, and pus, and black gore.

She has stripped herself of ego so you
can see right through her, the way she saw
beyond the angel, the candlegrease, the crumbs,
into the face of the God, pleading.

It is over, they are both at peace
though the pain of the one who lives
is almost unendurable and will last. She
has been asked again and has answered 'yes'.

IX   The Ring

She came out the back door, her grey hair
whisked by the winds, westering;
morning, the chores; sunlight

played like kittens with the flighty
hydrangea-leaf shadows across the yard;
her night-blue apron was riddled with stars,

the basin she carried old and dunted,
rust-flaked; yesterday's ashes
were whisked at once in a swirl about her

by the winds. She knelt on clay at the corner
of the pit and buried her hands deep
in the bucket, and found it, the ring that had slipped

from her finger, her body lessening; spoke
thanks, and her hands came clean-brushed
from the grey-silk kindliness of ash.

Otherwhere he waited, in dry clay, his flesh
become water and a golden ring
fallen loose from the mouldering bone.

X Slops

She crossed the yard in his hobnailed boots;
in her left hand, dragging her sideways,
the flaked enamel bucket filled with slops;
over skirts and cardigans the old man's coat;

she tipped the bucket out over a fence;
her old woman's face was pale, her skin
rough-stuff like an old mat; and all that yard
was caulked in ordure, and rains had washed

ash into every fissure. But she had gathered
the lily of quietness that grew on her own
restful plateaux: *you are all fair, beloved,*
your cheeks as pieces of the pomegranate.

She stood awhile, remembering, her breathing harsh,
and smiled, to know love is as strong as death.

Matrix

I took the pollack, fat from his predations
round the roots of the black rocks
and flopping now on the cliff ledge

and flung him high –

he shaped an arc of ecstacy through the air,
near-dead fish flying, and whooped
back again into the sea of love.

The Book of Love

Perhaps the words of poems
I am writing for you now
may drift before your consciousness
(long after you and I are ghosts)
like something almost asssuming
shape out of the long misting
of a long and misty day,
gone already but sustaining
among eternity's shiftless constellations:
that you and I have loved one another
across the in-between slow-motion times
we did not note exceptional, but were
the steadily sustaining everyday
alphabet of our togetherness.

Out of the Ordinary

A musty book is opening again
after winter silence: we are reminded
– tenebrae, passion, lamentations –
of the articles of perfection we aspire to.

Atlantic mists, as if responding,
shift as swathes of hooded spirits
gathering out of the west towards the east.
The daffodils are bent already

like rusty nails; the human soul
waits, raw as untreated timbers;
these days will stain the limbs
to a dark oak, our parentage being

elsewhere, Our Father. We travel,
like the mists, hesitant, within ourselves.

*

The roadside mudbank is a treasury
of primroses and violets; today
gales from the south-west have risen
and windmills on the far hill are high

agitated crosses. The hollow words of politics
have been spitting in our faces, and we pray,
Oh Lord, maker of the monstrous heavens
pity us in our long humiliation. Evening, rain

came hammering the window while we ate.
We offer (there are no exact words for this)
the corrupt bodies of the living, the incensed
bodies of the dead, wondering if the host –

its soft-sheen almond white – touches
the tongue in faith will it make it pure?

*

Friday dawned with uneasy sunshine,
cloud-shadows hurried on the meadows
and on the farthest hill a flock of sheep
moved restlessly. The white butterflies

are stirring, bluebells are nuns-of-Mary
in a huddle, seek shade from the demanding sun.
We re-enact the stations of human suffering;
we bury again the Christ in the garden tomb

in the convent cemetery where sisters lie
in tiny, ordered beds. Then by dusk
the martins had returned, a season's
end, a season's turn, the kingdom not yet come.

Midnight I stood, under the skylight,
till its small space was crowded out with stars.

*

Storms today, rushing from the south;
apple blossoms are perfect flakes of snow
with streaks of blood across them. This day,
like any ordinary day of our ordinary lives,

moves in the certainty of death and the longing
for rebirth. A mess of rooks is flung
randomly about; it is a day to empty sheds
of rubbish. In a corner of the meadow the bonfire,

a tyre sending black smoke heavenwards,
cardboard, a broken toy, old books, the wind
turning the pages over, the fire reading them.
Words, like small black butterflies

flung randomly about. The storm, knocking on the door
all hours this long, directionless day.

*

Dawn, blue-sky and virginal. In the cloister garden
the dying generations bind their will once more
to their absent God's. Each day the crumbs
gathered unto each day. The words of love,

suddenly erased from the world's page,
are just as suddenly rewritten. Magdalen,
out of her barrenness had found root, came
fox-cautious to an open door. Consent

is a movement of the will, an act
of foolishness, on earth as it is in heaven.
After the Sunday papers, the sherries,
after the feast of lamb, everything

will be as it was before, one year older. We
go on praying, deliver us from evil.

On Firm Ground

I had been watching bees among the foxglove thimbles
when I looked up and saw the hawthorns,
like Moses' bush in flames, but light with the fire
of a radiance whiter than white, and being conscious

of wars and weathers, wishing to hold in verse
something of the wonderful earth's outbreathing,
birds, for instance, like the golden oriole,
or the skittering sparrow, or the martins' flight

and wanting to honour along our roads and meadows
the birds-foot trefoil, the bitter vetch, the bladder campion,
the 'crúibín cait', the 'heath pea' and the 'white bottle',
I was imagining a Mass for all the dead and living

hurt by our culture of violence and untruth,
rehearsing names and memories and sacred words
like trinity, hosanna, requiem, when all at once
the colours, rhythms, music, the contained joy

converged to one softly moving presence, yours,
to one name, yours, and to one word, love,
and I breathed out quietly into the world's breathing
may the God of mountain pastures grant you peace.

Officium

Spare me Lord for my days fall like rubble.
What is man that you should magnify him;
why do you tender towards him your heart of love?
You visit him at dawn, waking his flesh to pain.
At dusk, in the urinary smell, his lower lip
hangs foolishly and words dreep out in spittle.
Why have you made him contrary to you,
labouring towards stick, walking frame, wheelchair,
where he sits staring and sucking on soft foods.
Can you erase his sins, empty them out like slops,
rebuild the crumbled scaffolding of his days?
The light burns dimly, fingers fidget on the sheets.
Today I will lie down in dust, and if tomorrow
you come in search of me, I am no more.

House Martins

Their round heads butting from the nest
they were three –
cowled and fledgling monks,
or novice topers with elbows
resting along the bar,
plump already and demanding,
the clean stillness of their egging
dumped.

Their nest was a miracle of mud and bird-spittle,
fastened like the church of Rome
to the highest niche available,
the world beneath them
despicable in soil and bird-shit –

but oh how the adults waltzed and tangoed down the air,
each one
a muscle perfected into flight,
impelled and catapulted to wear out
the sweetest season of their summering into care.

Soon
they will have fled the nest, a little
groggily, but proud as prelates, and you know again
in the secret place within that houses grace,
that everything beyond the rule and filthying of men
is whole, and holy, and unsoiled.

Acolyte

The wildness of this night – the summer trees
ripped and letting fall their still green leaves,
and the sea battering the coast
in its huge compulsion – seems as nothing

to the midnight chime from the black tower,
reiterating that all this tumult
is but the bones of Jesus in their incarnation.
I have flown today onto the island,

our small plane tossed like jetsam on the clouds;
I watched the girl, her mutilated brain,
the father urging, how her body rocked
in unmanageable distress, her fingers

bruising a half-forgotten doll; hers, too,
the Jesus-body, the Jesus-bones. Once
in early morning, the congregation
was an old woman coughing against echoes

and a fly frantic against the high window;
the words the priest used were spoken out as if
they were frangible crystal: *hoc – est – enim* ...
The Host was a sunrise out of liver-spotted hands

and I tinkled the bell with a tiny gladness;
the woman's tongue was ripped, her chin,
where I held the paten, had a growth of hairs;
her breath was fetid and the Host balanced

a moment, and fell. Acolyte I gathered
up the Deity, the perfect white of the bread
tinged where her tongue had tipped it; the
necessary God, the beautiful, the patience.

I swallowed it, taking within me
Godhead and congregation, the long obedience
of the earth's bones, and the hopeless urge
to lay my hands in solace on the world.

Gotland, July 2000

The Wild Meadow

I

I see him as an old man, snuff-dusted waistcoat
and faceless fob watch, late on his verandah
in unaltering perfection; there is no note

of birdsong or buzz of flies, no breeze or rain,
the light of dusk won't shift towards night; no one
to soothe his angers or ease away the strain

along his back. Non-being is a glaur that waits
malleable around him; should he shift
out of his stiffness his every shift creates

a universe, the glaur unsettling, viscid ripples
widening out from him where his being caught
on the thorns of movement, and his blood dripples;

the wild meadow of our universe marvellously wrought.

II

The old saints spoke of limbo and cast their children out
on headlands, into hidden graves, as if a child
– the wild meadow of our universe marvellously wrought –

could will its birthing and condemn its soul
in the dark womb. *Lead kindly light*, the old folks sang
and we were trudging out by asphodel and boghole

towards the ocean's edge where Clare Island's light
brushed over us with reassurance. Cliffs erode,
and who will sift the tiny bones from the white

bones of sailors cast nameless from the maelstrom? Made
other than God, we cannot yet lie faithfully
like driftspars on his caring, praising and unafraid

and watching to a far-off light that flashes fitfully.

III

Grandfather's the first death and it darkened the house
though in the year the old man died the lights went on
all over the island; we were drawing close

to the end of the middle ages. As they planted, like trees,
their foreign, creosoted poles, *nothing good*, he said,
will come of it; it was the end of islands, of rosaries,

of oil-lamp rituals. The old man folded himself away
as he had folded years before the RIC uniform
wrapped in its residue of bitterness. A new day

brightening; shadows banished from the night,
the women's faces lightened from their cares;
new Ireland, a new communion, the original light

summarily switched off on Eden's shore.

IV

We were trudging out by asphodel and boghole
– the stars on Mweelin's shoulder and a cold moon –
father and I; bog-oak roots were ghosts that stole

out of the past. We stalked the barnacle, their flight
beautiful down moonlit air, until he shot and one
flopped into the glaur. It was my fall too, out of delight

and ignorance, into error. On the quarry hill
we stood, breathtaking stars above, villages starbright
with Christ-birth candles; attend, let the heart fill

only with assent, like the stored wisdom of old trees –
but I heard the scream in the woodcore before the axeblow
echoed through the forests of space, the pleas

of small things hiding among grass-tufts of the meadow.

V

Winter too early; withholding grass; a blue light
flashing on a wall. After first love a man may grow
from roots of dream to an underbrush of loss. Peewit

flit and dip in the wild meadow, fog in the city,
dying-time; corridors stilled before the mardi gras
of visitors. She heard the tick tock of eternity,

her vegetative energies drippling down to nil.
A soul and body loved, dead now as glabrous stone,
the lover flung into fall. God had drawn out her will

and I went to seek out silences, the blood-flame
in the sanctuary, the thorned mearins of the meadow
where the ripples that were widening out of him

lay stagnant after the long dreep of the blood-flow.

VI

I stood at the shore's edge, arms extended
cruciform, like the cormorant with its wings out
to the watery sun. Silenced. All motive ended.

If you climb the sycamores in Mornington you may gaze
over field and estuary, towards the past: Newgrange,
Boyne waters; I could hide on summer days

owl-still, in leaf-shade. Gulls shriek in the breeze,
a tree trunk rots in the mudflats, desire
with no object had shaken me; night-whiskeys

and TV, a life diminished. Two hooded crows
lifted from the flotsam. But grace is offered freely
and I climbed down, expecting her, where the Boyne flows

out of constricting banks to lose itself in the sea.

VII

A blue Toyota van, Biscay, beaches stretched away
to the south; love under trees near Àvila,
birdsong everywhere, communion, wine-red clay;

as a man grows into grace the meridian lines of earth
hum a basso profundo psalmody of praise,
love recovering the distances back to God; rebirth

and reappraisal. At our feet a snipe creased
suddenly away, and a lark out of its secrecy as if
by stepping in the world a mist of song may be released

into the air. Nights sleep won't come, you strain
your body tighter into hers, being taught
that love grows stauncher having passed through pain,

the wild meadow of our universe marvellously wrought.

VIII

A small dog on the beach yaps against the waves;
a woman – *watch and assent* – is staring out to sea;
deep autumn day, sunlit like a forest clearing, the graves

gleam with a sort of peace. Five swans, in starlight,
passed effortfully over, wings freighted with mystery;
I thought of sacrament, of a young, surpliced acolyte

in the procession of the dead: *in paradisum deducant te …*
Another death, but no agony of blood this morning, only
the dignity of an old man in the old way

rehearsing ancient idioms. Advent has come,
the pain cycle; the heart and words for praise
are lacking among the wealth fetishes, the maelstrom,

they have abandoned us once more to decencies.

IX

These years we have been planting oaks; some day a child
may soar from the arms of one to the breast of another.
Cowslip, orchid, vetch, our pleasure is the wild

meadow, sheltering places of the lark; heartsease;
the breezes brush the grass with reassurance,
we have found together a degree of peace.

There was one child, East Timor, our time, who fled
terror through the night, who fell and died,
her body splayed where even her doll lay spread

in cruciform shape. Our lives are fragile as the thyme
and celandine, all of us lacking wholeness in our days:
cormorants, militias, God. Attempt the ordering of rhyme.

Attend, be guardian. Love, and offer praise.

For the Record

Cat
had worked the angled places
out beyond the kitchens of old flats,
hungry, exultant, obedient always

to cat-instincts, trammelled yet free,
of rust colour and ash-bucket grey,
professional with mouse and sparrow and flea;
kissed the midnight shadows and sprayed

importance on the shrubberies, and ran
disdaining domesticity. Thus –
till a car thudded over it and drove on;
cat was hurtling, and its impulse

carried across the street where it hauled
(I write it pityingly) its crushed
hind legs over a wall
and in under drippling bushes.

Silent and intent it sucked pain
into failing lungs, shivering, till a low, scared
wail of agony began. A time, and again
silence. Then it bared

perfect jungle-teeth in a sneer,
juddered once, and died. Here,
in this world's suffering, my few tears
of incomprehension and pity and fear

make no difference. Write,
recording angel, this was full cat, grown
perfect in wilderness, that tonight
was miserably brought down.

Fantasy in White

Over the brimming acres of wild meadow
the white butterflies, in a silent storm
of winged snowflakes, were fluttering
through their extravagant mating dance;
in this our fractured time and world-space
those of us who know ourselves to be broken
rejoiced in a moment of purest wonder;
where sin abounds there grace abounds the more.
By evening, absence had settled on the meadow
as after the exhalation of a deep-drawn breath,
one high star chilling in a grey, bleak sky;
imperceptibly the fall had come
and we turned once more towards the dark,
the white soul weighted in its winter boots.

Runt Bird

Today the adult birds
were inveigling the young from their nest;
come on in, they were calling, the sky is lovely.
The last, the smallest, came

fluttering downwards like an autumn leaf.
I hold it now forever, small as the human heart,
certainly as scared, and its innocent claws
cling to my manflesh. If I fling it into air

it may soar like brother Icarus for one
glorious moment, or fall
on the hard earth where cat and magpie
will be busy in the rutted slaughtering-places

and I must tell myself again that this
is runt bird, incapable,
and that the universe that claims us
thrusts on, beautiful and without compassion.

Scandal

Who said you have to rend your bones
or shred your soft flesh for sainthood?
When you go hankering after beauty

that you must pluck your eyes clean out?
You may be certain only
of the demands of gravity

and of the straining of the soul towards flight.
The roadside ditch is passionate now
with blackberries, and the pimpernel

has broken through the tarmac; and you –
what are you doing with your one life?
When the air is scanted you remember breathing;

when the words gag you remember truth;
when the heron lifts – beautiful and ungainly –
misprising your approach, remember how the world

was whole and wholesome once as it slipped
out from the fingers of its proud father
down into your care.

From a Far Country

Space, this sunbright autumn day
between rains; a beech hedgerow
ochre-gold and amber and tender-green,
stands classical in its fetchedness; the holly

rises to a clear sky, its clutch of berries
still and redolent; moments you touch
the equitable pulsing of the earth; mostly
our world is a high stone-studded door

and there is no way through; but, through,
God is at home in his and our suffering
and it is we who dawdle, language-lost,
in a far country we call our own;

He is beyond horizons and beyond beyond,
unviable, impossible, but still we stand
on a sunbright autumn day and breathe
with satisfaction the green word: *home*.

The Virgin's Song

(adapted from a fourteenth-century poem)

Jesu beloved –
son most dear,
on a wretched bed
you are lying here;

it grieves me, grieves me so;

your cradle a stone
cattle-byre where
ox and ass alone
may stumble near;

it grieves me, grieves me so.

But Jesu beloved do not cry,
you will not come to harm –
here there is no danger nigh
and you'll sleep warm

though it grieves me, grieves me so;

no gown have I nor linen vest,
the cloths are ripped and old –
but lay your feet against my breast,
you'll feel no cold;

oh beloved, it grieves me so.

The Apotheosis of Desire

(Luke Ch. 7: 'And behold a woman who was a sinner in the city ... who came and stood behind at his feet, weeping. And she began to bathe his feet with her tears, and wiped them with her hair ...')

1

The motorway, pre-dawn, in sickly light;
a cruel misting of spray from night-travelling
articulated trucks; the stomach clenching; a fox
crossed before my lowered lights, its lovely wildness
undiminished. The airport was its own city

in a haze of lights. Everywhere we move we move
with shadows; empty escalators roll
with an iron muttering; coffee machines stand bright,
untempting. When we go on board, at last, we go
like pilgrims already weary. The runways, at dawn,

are wood-paths with bauble-lights. Soon
we are high into quickening sunlight, as if ignorant again
that underneath is another world more real, and less,
than this. I pray: that his hand
bear you safely over the abyss until you land

on that loveliest of shores. Our cruciform shadow
shifting on the clouds below, is haloed in rainbows;
we are eight miles high – the ascending Christ
would have been lost to view, ice
taking his Jewish beard and being. The high life,

whiskey, pretzels; ice cubes clinking in the glass.

2

I am defiled, frustrated by desire.
There were some attended to his words
to pick among them afterwards, like daws;

I consented, simply, without having understood.
God's are the domains of mystery, mine
the concerns of longing, the domains of flesh.

Now the frenzy of living has been set aside,
the frenzy of dying anticipated, my life
trapped amongst high-tide refuse. I am all

attention; vulnerable soul-flesh; out of shell.
I had heard the name, rumours, marvels, bastard; what
understanding could be possible? Save that he

consented to my being, as I to his.
I was hopeless for him, the longing
numbed as when I stood outside his tomb, despondent.

I sit in darkness, waiting; a flame
burns in the glass, lights my absorption, as if my hand
cupped a cold, smooth skull; I would flay my flesh

in punishment, but for the worth of my still black hair
and the pathos of male cravings. He loved me, too,
I saw, for a time, beyond both flame and darkness;

and what have I to show? Old bones knotted.

3

After years this, today, is the found land, this
the old tome of marvels, the debilitating life-ache.
A solitary boy, Jew-child, plays apart, his ball
thunking down the stone steps from the Rock;
a lizard, like a spill of oil, flicks itself

into a crevice as I shift under the heat. The Old City
is a sea in storm, history a stone ship, I find
little I can cling to. *It's Jihad*, Tibi said, *rules
are down, and listen! our orders come direct from God*;
there are funerals in Ramallah, and women wailing

out of Beit Jala, the smaller children gathering stones
for sling-shots. Here you can rent a cross of smoothly
planed wood; among the confusion of gods I find
tourist signs pointing the Via Dolorosa; I step
cautiously over my dreams, find kitsch, the Coca-Cola signs,

the overwhelming smell of spices and naked meat,
stalls rife with the junk of old piosity. Bring
your signature, your banker's card. If I could touch
something he had touched, some trace that he had stepped
on original clay. I stand back among the shadows,

wipe sweat from my brow, find little comfort.

4

We sat quietly on the wooden pier, lake water
lulling us. My head on his shoulder, his right hand
around me, left hand in mine. He turned, asking

'What are you thinking? Tell me.' And between
what I had been thinking, and the putting of it into words
was devastating territory I could not cross.

Out over the lake the sorrow-laden flight
of the flamingos; mallard were in dispute among the reeds,
a solitary heron, angular, discrete, stood near shore.

I was in love, and scared. He, too, was scared, violent
agitation and territories occupied; funerals in Ramallah
and women wailing. Man is flesh, the spirit

will not remain in him forever. I followed him;
I saw his blood dreep down onto the clay; I heard him scream
in agony and despair, like I do, inwardly. I listen

to footsteps of the pious go shush across the temple floor. I held
his flesh once more, dawn, blue-sky and virginal, the tomb
door open, but he urged me from him, into shadows. Now I touch

the cold stones in the Western Wall, remembering
the rush and wildness once of his love, wondering
what can my life give back to Christ for this my life.

Oh devious God, dweller in shadows, mercy on us, the afflicted.

5

They laid him on his mother's knees, like an old child,
face distorted, and slow dribbles of blood
along his Jewish beard; I touched the perfect quarter-moons

of his fingernails, the lifeline like a contour map of the sky.
She and I, silenced, holding the hurt back, the way you hold
your palm to your side to contain the suffering.

I had washed my tears into his feet, the bitterness
of renounced possession, human love prefiguring
death; I dried them with my hair; the devils in me

the violent eroticism of my love. They had handled him
with violence, their scourges, lances, nails; I loved him,
how can I then forgive, or be forgiven?

I make my way sometimes up that dirt track
where people jostled for a view; stones, his naked feet,
the gouts of blood that made a paste against the clay. Desire

has been an overwhelming force within me; now
I am a pigeon home to roost on a soiled window ledge.
I attend. They will bury me with those tight-packed

inside the crevices on the hill, my heart's desire
shrivelled to an olive stone. So much love
has been written out with a stick on the dry earth

waiting for the winds to whistle it away.

We have set it up so often, remembering, on the rough
wood of the cross, the body, bared. I came, seeking
the Jesus-body, the Jesus-bones. In the Church of the Holy
                                                    Sepulchre
someone was playing Bach, softly: *Jesu joy
of man's desiring* ... I stood in awe; candles about the tomb,

Madonna lilies high and innocent; this, at last,
is the centre of creation; from here
he lies to north and south, he lies to east
and west and is the compass in me and the draw, it is in him
ultimately, I will be earthed. I have been handling

only my own desires, and walk again, uncertain.
Between the crevices of the Western Wall, paper slips
hold prayers that make a mortar of human pleading.
The onion domes of the Church of St Mary Magdalene
stand certain against the sky on the Mount of Olives;

I thought of her, would speak with her, of that
virginal morning, that shifting, uncertain shadow.
A vapour trail passed, slowly, high across the perfect blue.
And then frenzy again, of airports. Star-flights. Half-sleep.
Pre-dawn and my own familiar coastline, the plane

shuddering in storm as we came back down to earth.

Recessional

Noon, and the world stilled, winter chill
waiting among crimson berries;
drops of sacred water on the dark

polished wood, the heady scent of incense,
attendants bundling ourselves up
in comfort. The body hidden,

we cling to the innocence of belief
we have a hold over the future.
The wild meadow has been scarified,

tractor wheels have gouged mud ruts across it,
the nests ploughed under. We watch
our tie to the past and future slip away from us

on its whispering castors. Tonight
under plotted geographies of the sky
the stars' spectacular deaths will occur

in silence, as if nothing at all were happening.
On the window sill, in a white jar,
the gladioli's extravagant *amen*.

Canticle

Sometimes when you walk down to the red gate
hearing the scrape-music of your shoes across gravel,
a yellow moon will lift over the hill;
you swing the gate shut and lean on the topmost bar
as if something has been accomplished in the world;
a night wind mistles through the poplar leaves
and all the noise of the universe stills
to an oboe hum, the given note of a perfect
music; there is a vast sky wholly dedicated
to the stars and you know, with certainty,
that all the dead are out, up there, in one
holiday flotilla, and that they celebrate
the fact of a red gate and a yellow moon
that tunes their instruments with you to the symphony.